The Sensible Guide to Key Terminologies in Project Management

Featuring the 500

Most Commonly Used Words

Brian Williamson ▪ Te Wu

iExperi Press ▪ New Jersey

PMOAdvisory.com
Management Consulting with A Social Conscience®

The Sensible Guide to Key Terminologies in Project Management:
Featuring the 500 Most Commonly Used Words

Authors: Brian Williamson and Te Wu
Contributor: Estee Wu
Publisher: iExperi Press

Published in the United States
ISBN-13: 978-1-941913-09-3
ISBN-10: 1-941913-09-1

Version 1.0
Printed by CreateSpace, a DBA of On-Demand Publishing LLC

Table of Contents

PREFACE VII

ABOUT THE AUTHORS IX

ABOUT PROJECTMANAGEMENT.CO XI

ABOUT PMO ADVISORY.. XIII

TERMS (0-9, A-Z).. 1

    0-9.. 1
    A 2
    B... 11
    C... 19
    D 36
    E... 41
    F... 47
    G 53
    H 56
    I.. 57
    K... 61
    L... 63
    M 67
    N 71
    O 73
    P... 77
    Q 97
    R... 100
    S... 112
    T... 128
    U 133
    V... 134
    W 136

COMMON PROJECT MANAGEMENT FORMULAS 139

    EARNED VALUE FORMULAS 139
    FINANCIAL FORMULAS.. 143
    OTHER IMPORTANT FORMULAS... 144

FOR OUR READERS 145

SPECIAL OFFERS 147

DEDICATION

To all project professionals who work tirelessly to deliver projects on time, within budget, and to a level of quality that meets or exceeds client expectations.

Preface

Both authors of this publication have started their careers as accidental project managers. Both of us embarked on the path to project management without truly understanding the term. Yet, step by step and company and company, we both progressed steadily from entry-levels to becoming professionals. Along the way, we have witnessed many failed projects and even experienced a few disasters. But through them, we learned and moved beyond them.

One of the key problems with the practice of project management is the language itself. Words have meanings, but unless a concerted effort is taken to align these words, they often carry different meanings to different people. The problem exponentially intensifies as project teams, organization size, and project complexity increase. This planted the seed for the two of us to tackle this challenge.

Since the founding of PMO Advisory in 2012, the discipline of project management has been evolving quickly. As we create and deliver more courses for organizations that make a greater impact, our earlier concern with words and their meaning intensified. It became self-evident that we need a compilation of the common terms to enable better communication. Thus, the authors worked closely to assemble this terminology guide in which we carefully describe the 500 most common terms based on the latest practices, and we made efforts to align this with other global vocabularies such as those from the PMI lexicon and ISO Technical Committee 258 terminologies.

We hope that project practitioners will use this guide as another resource to develop a better and more insightful understanding of the important project management terminologies and that organizations use this guide to promote a common understanding among its employees.

About the Authors

Brian Williamson is an expert in the discipline of strategic portfolio, program, and project management focused on transforming organizational performance to create a new relationship between business, society, the environment, capital, and purpose. He is an expert in business analysis, strategic planning, leading transformational change, and helping organizations align their portfolios to purpose.

Brian is among the few people globally to hold all the renewable certifications from the Project Management Institute; is the 2018 recipient of the prestigious *PMI Eric Jenett Project Management Award of Excellence;* is a Chartered Project Professional (ChPP) and Fellow with the Association for Project Management; and holds the designation of ITIL® Expert in IT Service Management from Axelos. He is a Certified Fraud Examiner (CFE) by the Association of Certified Fraud Examiners (ACFE), and has received extensive training in Six Sigma. Brian holds two Masters Degrees from Polytechnic University, New York: Management of Technology (MoT) and Information Systems Engineering (ISE); a Bachelor of Science Degree from Teikyo-Post University in Waterbury CT; and an Associate Degree in Specialized Business from the Art Institute of Philadelphia. Brian is presently pursuing his Doctor of Education (Ed.D.) in Leadership and Learning in Organizations at Vanderbilt University.

Dr. Prof. Te Wu is the founder and CEO of PMO Advisory LLC, a professor with Montclair State University in New Jersey and China Europe International Business School, and an active volunteer with the Project Management Institute, along with being a member of the U.S. Technical Advisory Group 258 which represents the United States on the ISO Technical Committee 258 for Project, Program, and Portfolio.

Te has more than 25 years of experience in project management and management consulting. He worked with industry leaders such as KPMG, Accenture, Oracle, Kraft, Standard and Poor's, Chase Bank, Corning Incorporated, and LexisNexis. He is an expert at implementing transformative change, enterprise resource planning (ERP), master data management (MDM), data analysis, and process optimization and simulation. For the past 16 years, Te has also held professorships at multiple universities teaching international business, general management, organizational change, and project management. These include Stevens Institute of Technology, Touro Graduate School of Business, Montclair State University, and China Europe International Business School (CEIBS).

Te is one of few professionals worldwide certified in Portfolio (PfMP), Program (PgMP), Project (PMP), Risk (PMI-RMP) Management. In his spare time, he is working on a range of publications and research. Te also serves as a board member and in various advisory capacities for multiple educational institutions.

About ProjectManagement.co

ProjectManagement.co is an information portal dedicated to the project management professional. The goal is to provide current, relevant, and quality information that would enable professionals to learn, collaborate, and grow. The key features of this website, some of which are still under construction, include the following:

1. Provide relevant and timely content, such as book reviews, research highlights, latest news, best practices and insights, and other valuable information;
2. Interviews with professionals to gain perspectives, knowledge, and experiences;
3. Research studies to promote more effective project management by bridging a significant between practice and ivory tower;
4. Events including webinars, symposiums, conferences, and training; and
5. Promotional offers to free or discounted courses, tools, and other valuable services.
    a. To start, the terms in this lexicon is available for free to all registered professionals.

ProjectManagement.co provides these plus more for free to registered professionals. For more information or just to see it for yourself, visit www.projectmanagement.co.

About PMO Advisory

PMO Advisory was founded on the simple idea that sound project management will literally change the world by getting the *right* things done, better, faster, more cost effective, and with greater stakeholder satisfaction. And PMO Advisory wants to be in the middle of that excitement, striving to add more value to the discipline as it strengthens and expands by providing high quality training and consulting services. As a PMI Global Registered Education Provider (PMI R.E.P. #4172), PMO Advisory is one of the few firms that provide training and certification boot camps for portfolio management (PfMP)®, program management (PgMP)®, project management (PMP® and CAPM®), agile project management (PMI-ACP)®, risk management (PMI-RMP)®, project management office (PMO), organization change management (OCM), and strategic business execution (SBE).

Today, PMO Advisory is a leader in project management training and consulting, and we blend training with consulting to deliver powerful and effective solutions to address unique problems.

For more information, visit us at www.pmoadvisory.com.

As a reader of this book, you are qualified to access our monthly webinar and earn one PDU for free. Please see "Special Offer" at the end of the book.

Terms (0-9, A-Z)

0-9

Term	Description
80/20 Rule	Formerly known as the Pareto Principle, this is a statistical rule of thumb which states that 80 percent of a target effect comes from 20 percent of sources or causes for a particular event or activity. For example, 80% of stakeholder challenges come from 20% of the stakeholders. Also see Pareto Principle.

A

Term	Description
Acceptance Test-Driven Development (ATDD)	A method of defining and creating acceptance tests prior to delivery that emphasizes collaborative development of acceptance test criteria.
Accuracy	An assessment of correctness used in estimation and quality management systems. Also see Precision.
Active Listening	A communication technique in which an individual pays close attention to the verbal communication from stakeholders. By listening carefully, analyzing the content, and clarifying the underlying meanings, active listening will enhance communication and reduce ambiguity.
Activity	A basic unit of work in project planning that serves as the basis for scheduling, resource planning, and budgeting. An activity usually comprises numerous related tasks, which must be completed in order for the activity to be considered as complete.

Term	Description
	Also see Assignment, Task, and Work Breakdown Structure.
Activity Code	Activity codes represent a specific value that is assigned to an activity. These codes are unique and are utilized for keeping track of and making a logical sequence of all activities. Also see Activity Identifier and Activity Label.
Activity Identifier	A particular identifying value assigned to an activity that is unique and is used to discern each activity. Also see Activity Code and Activity Label.
Activity Label	A description for a specific activity consisting of a brief label or phrase that is consigned to that activity for assisting in differentiating them from one another. Also see Activity Code and Activity identifier.
Activity List	A list of project or program activities that are usually sequenced and planned for implementation.

Term	Description
	Also see Activity.
Actual Cost (AC)	The true costs of all activities accrued during the time period of interest. Also see Budget at Completion (BAC), Earned Value (EV), Estimate at Completion (EAC), Estimate to Complete (ETC), and planned Value (PV).
Adaptive Life Cycle	See Agile Life Cycle.
Adhocracy	A management approach based on the principles of self-management and self-organization. The hallmark of adhocracy is its informal, dynamic, and adaptable structure and its ability to change quickly and organically as needs arise. Philosophically, it is the opposite of bureaucracy.
Agile	A management philosophy that focuses on value and customer interactions where requirements evolve through the collaborative effort of self-organizing cross-functional teams. The term was popularized in the Agile Manifesto.

Term	Description
Agile Certified Practitioner (PMI-ACP®)	Project Management Institute's professional-level certification for project professionals who specialize in agile approaches and methods. This certification is designed to indicate the individual's ability to lead agile projects including the application of agile management concepts, processes, tools, and techniques. Unlike many other agile-related certifications, PMI-ACP is methodology neutral.
Agile Coach	An agile coach helps a team or an individual to adapt and improve agile methods and practices. The coach helps people rethink and change the way they go about requirements gathering and development.
Agile Life Cycle	A type of project life cycle that is designed to embrace change through incremental implementation cycles. Also known as the "agile approach" or "agile method", the adaptive life cycle requires a high degree of ongoing stakeholder involvement often with fixed time and resources. Also see Incremental Life Cycle, Iterative Life Cycle, Life Cycle,

Term	Description
	Predictive Life Cycle, and Product Life Cycle.
Agile Manifesto	An original proclamation that articulates four key values and twelve principles that software developers should use to guide their work.
Agile Mindset	An agile mindset is the set of attitudes supporting an agile working environment. These include respect, collaboration, improvement and learning cycles, pride in ownership, focus on delivering value, and the ability to adapt to change.
Agile Practitioner	Someone who practices the agile approach to project or product delivery. Also see Agile Manifesto and Agilest.
Agile Principles	Essential "truths" that support the teams in the implementation and execution of the agile processes. According to the Agile Manifesto, there were twelve principles of agile delivery.
Agile Unified Process	An approach of a simple and understandable way of setting up business applications by making use of agile processes and techniques. Agile

Term	Description
	Unified Process is a simplified version of the Rational Unified Process (RUP).
Agilest	An advocate of the Agile approach to delivery, which includes an enthusiasm for agile design, agile development, agile delivery, and agile methodology. The person also embraces the core principles of the Agile Manifesto. Also see Agile Manifesto and Agile Practitioner.
Analogous Estimating	A technique for the estimation of a range of project measures largely based on historical data of similar activities or projects. The project measures can include cost, duration, resources, and scope. Also see Bottom-up Estimating, Definitive Estimating, Parametric Estimating, Program Evaluation and Review Technique (PERT), and Three-Point Estimating.
Anti-Pattern	Common ineffective solutions to a known pattern of work that are inherently flawed. Project teams should identify these failed patterns to avoid ineffective solutions.

Term	Description
Apportioned Effort	Energy or effort applied proportionally on project-related activities that are not readily divisible into discrete efforts. For example, an enterprise risk management team in a company provide their expertise across a range of projects in a PMO. This apportioned effort is proportionally distributed across the projects in the PMO. The contrasting to apportioned effort is discreet effort. Also see Apportioned Effort, Discrete Effort, and Level of Effort.
Artifact	A deliverable or work product that is created in order to describe a system, solution, or state of an enterprise. Examples of artifacts include the Business Case, Charts, Diagrams, Project Charter, Requirement Documents, or Stakeholder Analysis.
Assignment	A defined unit of work that has the following attributes: start and end dates, clear objectives and outcomes, people or roles assigned to work on it, and associated performance metrics.

Term	Description
	Also see Activity, Task, and Work Breakdown Structure.
Assumption	An aspect of the planning process considered to be certain, real, or true without significant demonstration or proof.
Audit	A process of evaluating the portfolio, program, and project management processes and activities with the generally established or pre-agreed rules, principles, guidelines, and requirements.
Authority	A formal power granted by the sponsoring organization to make project, program, and portfolio decisions in regard to resources, funding, tradeoff, and other key decisions.
Authorization	The process of giving or declining permission by an authority to perform work, such as resource allocation, funding approvals, initiating projects, etc., in the interest of the organization. In program management or portfolio management, this is the management process of formally approving

Term	Description
	components within a program or portfolio.
Automated Code Quality Analysis	Automatic detection of a broad range of potential bugs, along with harmful or non-optimized code.

B

Term	Description
Backlog	See Product Backlog.
Backlog Refinement	The progressive and continuous effort of keeping the backlog updated, organized, and clean. The process typically starts at the end of one sprint to make sure the backlog is ready for the next sprint. Formerly known as backlog grooming.
Backward Pass	The calculation of late start dates and late finish dates for the "schedule activities" portions that are typically in a critical path method. This is determined by calculating the scheduled end date of the project and working backward through the schedule model. Also see Forward Pass.
Balanced Scorecard	A system of reporting key performance indicators (KPIs) for a project, program, or portfolio. The goal is to provide a comprehensive picture of the underlying endeavor by selecting a few

Term	Description
	KPIs that are the most impactful or informative.
Baseline	An approved set of project work to be tracked and compared with the actual results. Any change to the baseline requires a formal change management authorization. Also see Cost Baseline, Performance Measurement Baseline, Schedule Baseline, and Scope Baseline.
Behavior-Driven Development (BDD)	See Broken Comb.
Benefit	The tangible and intangible gains such as financial advantages, new products, competitive capabilities, and valuable additions received by the stakeholders and the organization as a result of the program. Also see Value.
Benefit-Cost Ratio (BCR)	An economic ratio used to summarize the overall relationship between the relative costs versus benefits of projects, programs, or portfolios. BCR of greater than 1 indicates the net positive benefit.

Term	Description
	Also see Internal Rate of Return, Net Present Value, and Payback Period.
Benefits Analysis and Planning	A benefit management stage that includes activities to create and establish the program benefits management plan, framework, and metrics. The output from this planning is used throughout the program execution to monitor and control program components to enable a greater likelihood of achieving program benefits.
Benefits Delivery	A benefit management stage that focuses on the implementation of program activities to build and deliver the planned benefits.
Benefits Identification	A benefit management stage that identifies the program benefits. This is achieved by analyzing and evaluating the existing information such as the program business case, organization strategies, internal and external factors that impact the program.
Benefits Management	A set of deliberate processes of managing an endeavor's planned benefits, intended outcomes, and

Term	Description
	results throughout the project, program, or portfolio life cycle.
Benefits Management Plan	A formal document that explains the process for identifying, defining, delivering, and managing benefits and their sustainment throughout the project, program, or portfolio life cycle.
Benefits Realization	A delivery process of attaining benefits incrementally throughout the life cycle of projects, programs, and portfolios.
Benefits Register	A repository that captures project, program, and portfolio benefits that are identified initially during the early phases of the endeavor but should be updated throughout the endeavor's life cycle.
Benefits Sustainment	The final stage of a project, program, or portfolio in which the benefits attained during the endeavor are now proactively managed on an ongoing basis to achieve the desired benefits.
Benefits Transition	A stage of a project, program, or portfolio in which the benefits attained during the execution are being transitioned to an operational entity for the ongoing management of benefits.

Term	Description
Blended Agile	Usage of two or more agile elements, frameworks, methods, or techniques concurrently.
Blocker	A person or an obstacle that impedes the progress of a project. Also see Impediment.
Bottom-up Estimating	An estimating technique whereby the Work Breakdown Structure's lower-level tasks and activities are aggregated in order to estimate the cost or duration of a project. This technique is generally more accurate than analogous and parametric estimating. Also see Analogous Estimating, Definitive Estimating, Parametric Estimating, Program Evaluation and Review Technique (PERT), and Three-Point Estimating.
Brainstorming	A group creativity technique used to gather information, often for solving problems by identifying threats, determining root causes, and generating options and solutions with the help of subject matter experts and specialists.
Broken Comb	A specialist having many skill specializations as required by the team.

Term	Description
	Also see I-Shape and T-Shape.
Budget	The approved estimate for the total project, program, or portfolio costs that is inclusive of the cost of all planned components. It also includes the total amount of component cost estimates, contingency reserves, and sometimes the management reserve as well.
	Also see Contingency Reserve and Management Reserve.
Budget at Completion (BAC)	The total budget of the work to be performed, inclusive of all people and non-people costs.
	Also see Actual Cost (AC), Earned Value (EV), Estimate at Completion (EAC), Estimate to Complete (ETC), and planned Value (PV).
Burn Rate	The pace in which projects, programs, or portfolios spend the funding available.
Burndown Chart	Typically used in Scrum, a burndown chart is a graphical representation that displays the amount of work left against the remaining time.

Term	Description
Burnup Chart	Typically used in Scrum, a burnup chart is a graphical representation that displays the amount of work completed against the planned release of a product.
Business Case	A feasibility report for projects, programs, and portfolios used to establish the rationale for undertaking the endeavor.
Business Execution	The act and process of delivering the anticipated outcomes, results, and benefits by balancing action, activities, and investments with analysis, planning, and collaboration with key stakeholders and project teams.
Business Requirement Documents (BRD)	A document that identifies and lists all the business level requirements of a project. In the Software Development Life Cycle (SDLC), business requirements are further refined, analyzed, and transformed into functional requirements. Also see Functional Requirement.
Business Transformation	A change management scheme that is aimed at aligning people, processes, and the technological initiatives of an organization more closely with its

Term	Description
	mission, vision, strategic goals, and organizational objectives.
Buy-in	The management process of authorizing components within projects, programs, and portfolios. The authorization typically involves the assignment of funding and allocation of resources.

C

Term	Description
Cadence	The rhythm of work during the project or program execution phase.
Capability Assessment	An in-depth examination of the organization's resources and capabilities.
Capacity and Capability Analysis (CCA)	An analysis technique designed to evaluate the resources (human, finance, technology, machinery) of an organization required to implement projects, programs, or portfolios.
Capacity Management	The processes for managing and optimizing project, program, and portfolio resources between the demands of existing work and resource requirements to fulfill the needs of the initiative.
Capacity Planning	A planning analysis technique to determine the resource demand needed to meet the requirements of the endeavor.
Category	A pre-specified grouping or classification of ideas and components

Term	Description
	that share similar attributes or common objectives.
Cause and Effect Diagram / Ishikawa Diagram	A tool to uncover deeper and more probable root causes of issues by creating illustrative diagrams. This is often drawn in the shape of a fish, with the head as the main problem and the central spine as the main and potential causes of problems. The spine can be organized by major and smaller bones, each representing small units or components of the main problems. Often used in quality management, this tool can be used to decompose larger issues, risks, and other challenges.
Certified Associate in Project Management (CAPM®)	Project Management Institute's entry-level certification for project professionals who command the basic knowledge of project management concepts including knowledge areas, processes, tools, and techniques.
Change Agent	A person or group that encourages and motivates others to accept or embrace organizational change related to the project, program, or portfolio. Also see Change Champion.
Change Champion	A person or group, typically in leadership roles, that actively supports,

Term	Description
	facilitates, and promotes others to accept or embrace change related to the project, program, or portfolio. Also see Change Agent.
Change Control	The process of managing project change, including key documents, deliverables, and baselines associated with the initiative. The process includes the identification, documentation, change assessment, and decision-making. Also see Change Control Board, Change Control System, and Change Request.
Change Control Board	A formal group of individuals within a portfolio, program, or project structure, who have been commissioned to evaluate and recommend final decisions regarding if and when any particular changes are to be made in terms of scope, schedule, cost, or associated quality of work identified in the charter. Also see Change Control, Change Control System, and Change Request.
Change Control System	A set of processes, procedures, and tools for conducting change control.

Term	Description
	Also see Change Control, Change Control Board, and Change Request.
Change Fatigue	A behavioral or emotional condition in which a person suffers from frequent bombardment or ineffectiveness of organization change management. Change fatigue can be caused by many factors, some of which include poor leadership, weak communication, unnecessary stress, unclear goals and objectives, and unspecific benefits for the individual or the organization. Also see Change Resistance and Resistance Mitigation.
Change Impact	Consequences of change as a result of implementing projects, programs, or portfolios. Examples of change impacts include organizational structure, business processes, technology and automation, risk management, governance, products and innovation, and customer satisfaction. Also see Change Readiness and Change Resiliency.

Term	Description
Change Management	The techniques, tools, and processes for managing the people side of the organizational change in order to accomplish the strategic business objectives.
Change Readiness	Perception of organizational preparedness to adopt change successfully, typically measured by stakeholder judgment. Change readiness considers multiple drivers of change impact such as organizational cultural, individual or team commitment, and organization's capacity to support change. Also see Change Impact and Change Resiliency.
Change Request	A proposition to modify a previously agreed upon baseline, document, or deliverable. Also see Change Control, Change Control Board, Change Control System, and Change Request.
Change Resilience	An organization's capability of overcoming obstacles to ultimately adopt and accept change.

Term	Description
	Also see Change Impact and Change Readiness.
Change Resistance	Opposition or defiance toward change that may occur in projects, programs, or portfolios that require some level of organizational change. Change resistance can occur for many reasons, such as perceived (or real) unreasonable of change. Other reasons include change fatigue or poor change management. Also see Change Fatigue and Resistance Mitigation.
Charter	A document that includes the specification and authorization pertaining to the structure of a specific project, program, or portfolio. Issued by a sponsor, this document also associates the endeavor to the goals and objectives of the organization. The charter grants formal authorization to the project, program, or portfolio manager to guide and oversee activities within the context of organizational, contractual, and third-party resources. The Program or Portfolio Charter also connects the strategic goals and

Term	Description
	objectives of the organization with the endeavor.
Code of Accounts	A tool for assigning a code made from letters, numbers, or a combination of the two to each component on the work breakdown structure (WBS).
Collective Code Ownership	A collaboration technique in which the code is owned collectively by the team. By emphasizing team ownership and accountability, team members are empowered to make responsible changes that can accelerate the developmental effort.
Colocation (colo)	A locational strategy which emphasizes placing team members in the same or nearby physical location for the benefit of enhanced communication, improved working relationships, and increased benefits.
Commitment Curve	A curve that illustrates the stages through which individuals pass as they confront change. A typical curve starts with an initial shock and surprise by the change that deteriorates into a low point of despair before climbing upward toward rationalization and (hopefully) acceptance and commitment.

Term	Description
Communication Channel or Medium	A communication channel or medium is the method and manner that supports the delivery of communication from the sender to the receiver. Typically, there are two dimensions: formal versus information and verbal versus written. For example, a casual discussion is a verbal and informal communication. An approved project charter is a written and formal communication.
Communication Management	The process of developing and implementing a project, program, or portfolio communication management plan, including the processes the creation, collection, dissemination, storage, retrieval, and disposition of information.
Communication Management Plan (for Program, Project, or Portfolio)	A supporting plan within the overall Management Plan (e.g. Portfolio, Program, or Project) that defines the communication activities, tasks, responsible parties, and recipients of the information. The plan is also used to evaluate the effectiveness of the Communication Management Strategy.
Communication Matrix	A communication matrix is an evaluation tool used to determine the

Term	Description
	optimal communication channel for a specific group of stakeholders, in order to achieve the desired communication outcome.
Communication Strategy	A communication strategy is a plan to share information effectively and to achieve the desired goals in support of project, program, and portfolio management.
Compliance	Conformance to a rule, standard, directive, requirement, or set of guidelines.
Component	A discrete unit of work within a larger endeavor required to support the overall goal, objectives, and strategic imperatives of the organization. For example, within a program, a component can be projects and sub-programs. For portfolios, a component can be projects, programs, and sub-portfolios within the portfolio.
Component Proposal	A formal or informal plan, business case, or feasibility study that makes a recommendation in support of advancing a component (e.g. project, program, or portfolio).

Term	Description
Component Report (Program or Portfolio)	Performance reports of a portfolio or program providing the status by the component managers.
Configuration Management System (CMS)	A set of procedures taken into account for monitoring and controlling changes in project, program, or portfolio artifacts.
Conflict	Escalating disagreements arising from differences in priorities, processes, and personal or organizational views and values. If left alone, conflicts can spiral into larger conflicts with vicious negative cycles feeding and intensifying themselves.
Conformance	Delivering results or outcomes that are within the agreed parameter or limit of acceptability. This term is often used in quality management, and it refers to the acceptance of a deliverable.
Constraint	A factor that limits the options or establishes the boundaries for managing a project, program, portfolio, activity, or process.
Context Diagram	A visual representation of product scope depicting a system within the business and its interactions with

Term	Description
	people, related processes, and other systems.
Contingency	An uncertain event or occurrence that may affect the project, program, and portfolio execution in which the project professional should consider setting aside a reserve should the event occur.
Contingency Plan	A preconceived plan that describes ensuing actions should some predetermined trigger conditions occur. Also see Fallback Plan.
Contingency Reserve	An active risk response strategy in which time or funds are proactively set aside to manage the known project, program, or portfolio risks. Also see Management Reserve, Project Budget, and Reserve.
Continuous Delivery	A framework and practice that enables the frequent delivery of incremental enhancements and fixes to customers. This is achieved through the use of small batches of work and usually with the aid of automation technology for release management.

Term	Description
Continuous Integration	A framework and practice in which the team member's work products are frequently and continuously integrated and validated in the master product.
Contract	A legally binding agreement between the seller and buyer that obligates the seller to provide products and services, and the buyers to pay per the negotiated agreements and terms.
Control Account	Used as a management control point which involves the integration of budget, scope, schedule, and actual cost and their comparison with earned value for the measurement of performance.
Corrective Action	Any activity or action intended for realigning the course of a particular project or task with the previously established project, program, or portfolio management plan. Also see Preventive Action.
Cost Baseline	An approved plan established once a thorough budget is developed and is set as the parameter of comparison for actual performance status. Also see Baseline, Performance

Term	Description
	Measurement Baseline, Schedule Baseline, and Scope Baseline.
Cost Management Plan	A document outlining the activities and criteria which must be included as part of a Project Management Plan in terms of controlling, structuring, and planning the costs associated with the initiative. According to the *PMBOK® Guide*, this is a component plan within the project management plan.
Cost of Quality (COQ)	The cost associated with managing and delivering a quality product or service that includes quality planning, quality control, and quality assurance. Also see Quality Planning, Quality Control, and Quality Assurance.
Cost Performance Index (CPI)	Earned value management measure designed to evaluate project or program cost efficiency. It is expressed as a ratio of earned value (EV) to actual cost (AC). *Formula: CPI = EV / AC* Also see Schedule Performance Index (SPI).

Term	Description
Cost Plus Award Fee Contracts (CPAF)	A contract type that involves payments to the seller for all agreed upon work and cost of that work, plus an award fee that represents the seller's profits.
Cost Plus Fixed Fee Contract (CPFF)	A contract type that involves payments to the seller for all agreed upon work and cost of that work, plus a pre-negotiated profit margin for the seller.
Cost Plus Incentive Fee Contract (CPIF)	A contract type that involves payments to the seller for all agreed upon work and cost of that work, plus an incentive fee for accomplishing a pre-defined goal, such as meeting a quality standard or completing work early.
Cost Plus Percentage of Cost (CPPC)	A type of fee structure that involves payments to the seller for all agreed upon work and cost of that work, plus a pre-specified percentage of the cost as profit for the seller.
Cost Variance (CV)	Measured as the difference between Earned Value (EV) and the Actual Cost (AC), it is intended to express the amount of budget surplus or deficit at a given point in a project or program. *Formula: CV = EV - AC* Also see Schedule Variance (SV).

Term	Description
Cost-Benefit Analysis	In-depth analysis of the expected costs and the benefits for the determination of the required action. Traditionally included as part of a business case.
Cost-Reimbursable Contract	A contract type that involves payments to the seller for all agreed upon work and cost of that work, plus an additional fee representing the seller's profit.
Crashing	A scheme for schedule compression intended to decrease the total period of time for the minimum incremental cost by adding additional resources to the task or activity. Also see Fast Tracking and Schedule Compression.
Critical Chain Method	A scheme for scheduling that enables placement of buffers on any schedule path of a project to incur the limited uncertainties and resources of a project.
Critical Path	The longest activity sequence of a project or program that determines the shortest possible duration to complete the endeavor.

Term	Description
	Also see Critical path Activity, Critical Path Method, and Near-Critical Path.
Critical Path Activity	The tasks that are set on the critical path in the schedule of the project. Also see Critical Path and Critical Path Method.
Critical Path Method (CPM)	A scheme used to determine the amount of scheduling flexibility and estimation of the minimum project duration within the schedule model on the logical network paths. Also see Critical Path and Critical Path Activity.
Critical Success Factor (CSF)	A factor or activity that is essential for the success of a project, program, portfolio, or organization. CSFs are often confused with Key Performance Indicators. CSFs are "causes" for success, while KPIs are indicators that measure the "effects" or "outputs" of striving toward that success. Also see Key Performance Indicator (KPI).
Cross-Functional Team	A team that is composed of professionals with a multitude of skills (e.g. functional, technical) required to

Term	Description
	work on more complex problems or endeavors.
Crystal Family of Methodologies	A collection of agile software development methods that emphasize the swift adaptability to a particular situation.
Culture	The system of values, behaviors, attitudes, and traditions that are often unspoken in an organization, which affects the planning and execution of projects, programs, and portfolios.
Current State	The current state refers to the current set of circumstances or conditions. Understanding the current state is important to evaluate the effort required to achieve the desired future state. Also see Future State.
Cutover	In software development, the process of moving from one system or environment to another as the software progresses from development and testing to eventual deployment or activation.

D

Term	Description
Daily Scrum	A short daily meeting in which the focus is primarily on removing impediments even though the meeting can also include a review of the previous day's work and improvement suggestions. Also known as a daily standup. Note: Even though the word "daily" appears in the name, in practice, there can be multiple daily scrum meetings as required by the project.
Daily Standup	See Daily Scrum
Data Date	The specific date on which the actual status and accomplishments of a project are taken into consideration.
Decision Tree Analysis	A scheme that involves calculation and diagrams, in order to analyze multiple options and the implications associated with them in the presence of uncertainty.
Decomposition	A planning scheme that deconstructs abstract work into smaller and more concrete components.

Term	Description
Defect Repair	Corrective action for the modification of a project component or product without changing the baseline.
Definition of Done (DoD)	A checklist that identifies all the agreed upon acceptance criteria for a deliverable or service. When fulfilled, the deliverable or service can be considered ready for release or use. Furthermore, the definition will specify how the user will determine if the work is acceptable, usually with respect to objective criteria.
Definition of Ready (DoR)	A user-centric checklist that identifies all of the agreed upon criteria in order to start work on a project, product, or deliverable.
Definitive Estimating	The cost estimate built from the detailed level analysis of tasks and activities, typically from a work breakdown structure of a project and program. Definitive estimates are the most accurate methods of estimation with a range of -5% to +10% of the predicted cost. Also see Analogous Estimating, Bottom-up Estimating, Parametric Estimating, Program Evaluation and

Term	Description
	Review Technique (PERT), and Three-Point Estimating.
Deliverable	Any distinct and unique element, product, item, or result that is developed for delivery at the completion of a particular project activity, component, task, or at the completion of the whole project.
Delphi Technique	A method of collecting data based on a consensus of subject matter experts (SMEs). The technique reduces bias in data gathering by using a trained facilitator who works with subjects anonymously to avoid undue influence on the outcome.
Dependency	See Logical Relationship.
DevOps Practices (DevOps)	A set of practices for Development and Operations with the goal of creating a smooth flow of development and delivery through deep collaboration between the development and operational teams.
Disciplined Agile (DA)	An agile framework based on simplified process decisions around iterative and modular solution delivery.
Discrete Effort	An activity or task that can be directly identified, traced and planned, and

Term	Description
	that is directly connected with the final completion of the deliverables as well as the work breakdown structure component. Also see Discrete Effort and Level of Effort.
Double Loop Learning	A learning process that not only analyzes the results of a process but also the underlying values and assumptions. As a result, the individual or team can better determine the root cause of the situation and devise better ways of managing the situation. Also see Single Loop Learning.
Duration (DU or DUR)	The total amount of time required to complete work such as a project, an activity, a task, an assignment, or a work breakdown structure component. Duration is expressed in a unit of time (e.g. years, months, weeks, days, hours, or minutes). Also see Effort.

Term	Description
Dynamic Systems Development Method (DSDM)	An agile delivery framework that balances traditional project planning with an iterative development approach.

E

Term	Description
Early Finish Date	The earliest possible point at which an activity may potentially be completed. This is calculated via the use of the known predictable scheduling constraints, as well as precisely integrating the data date as well as schedule network logic. Also see Early Start Date, Late Start Date, Late Finish Date, and Schedule Network Analysis.
Early Start Date	The earliest possible point at which the in-progress portions of a schedule activity may potentially be started. This is calculated via the use of the known predictable scheduling constraints, scheduling network logic, and the most up to date information about the project. Also see Early Finish Date, Late Start Date, Late Finish Date, and Schedule Network Analysis.

Term	Description
Earned Value (EV)	The specific and precise sum total of accomplished project work on the basis of the authorized budget. Also see Actual Cost (AC), Budget at Completion (BAC), Estimate at Completion (EAC), Estimate to Complete (ETC), and Planned Value (PV).
Earned Value Management (EVM)	The project management performance methodology that provides integrated management of scope, schedule, and resource measurements to evaluate a project and program performance and progress.
Effort	The quantifiable and specific count and/or measure of units of definable labor that are required for the completion of a work breakdown structure component, schedule activity or task, often expressed in weeks, days, or hours. Also see Duration.
Emotional Intelligence (EQ)	The interpersonal capability of working with people and teams through the process of identification, evaluation, and management of sentimentally charged situations. The five main

Term	Description
	components of EQ are Self-Awareness, Self-Regulation, Motivation, Empathy, and Social Skills.
Empathy Interview	A technique to identify a person's experience as a "focus", a space, a process, an objective, or an environment.
Enterprise Environmental Factors (EEF)	Conditions that are outside the immediate influence and control of the endeavor, and therefore, they are not under the immediate control of the project, program, or portfolio team. For example, this includes economic, legal, political, social, and technological factors.
Enterprise Project Management Office (EPMO)	A project management office (PMO) is responsible for the overall organizational project environment. The chief responsibilities vary, but they generally involve establishing and managing methodology, reporting, training, career management, providing decision support for upper management, and possibly leading organizational-wide projects, programs, and portfolios. EPMOs are sustained organizational units that are often cross-functional. In

Term	Description
	practice, an EPMO can exist at many levels in their respective organizations (e.g. Departmental, Product, Business Unit, Divisional, or Corporate level). Also see Project Management Office, Program Management Office, and Portfolio Management Office.
Estimate	A quantitative assessment of approximate project, program, or portfolio costs, resources, or duration.
Estimate at Completion (EAC)	Used for measuring the expected total cost of a particular work breakdown structure component or a scheduled activity, which is an addition of both the Estimate To Complete (ETC) and Actual Costs (AC) to date. *Formula: EAC = BAC / CPI or AC + ETC* Also see Actual Cost (AC), Budget at Completion (BAC), Earned Value (EV), Estimate to Complete (ETC), and planned Value (PV).
Estimate to Complete (ETC)	Used for measuring the anticipated or expected costs for completing the remaining project work. *Formula: ETC = EAC - AC*

Term	Description
	Also see Actual Cost (AC), Budget at Completion (BAC), Earned Value (EV), Estimate at Completion (EAC), and planned Value (PV).
Evaluation	The process of assessing options to determine the potential course of action. In portfolio management, for example, evaluation is the process of scorning components in support of making investment decisions.
Evolutionary Value Delivery (EVO)	An agile delivery approach that focuses on delivering the final product through a small but unique and valuable component to stakeholders. This is often credited with being the first true agile method.
Expected Monetary Value (EMV)	The weighted outcome of monetary analysis, typically involving the probabilities of achieving results. For example, a project has 50% chance of saving $1 million annually. The EVM is $0.5 million.

Term	Description
Extreme Programming (XP)	An agile software development technique with short release cycles that collectively lead to a better quality of software with enhanced responsiveness to varying demands of the clients.

F

Term	Description
Fallback Plan	An alternate set of available actions and tasks in the event that the primary plan needs to be abandoned because of issues, risks, or other causes. Also see Contingency Plan.
Fast Tracking	A scheme for schedule compression in which simultaneous phases or activities are performed concurrently instead of performing them in sequence for some part of the duration. See also Crashing and Schedule Compression.
Feature-driven Development	An agile software development method that focuses on deliver customer-driven features, especially those requirements that are small but valuable, incrementally.
Feedback Mechanisms	A method of providing value-added and preferably constructive evaluation of a past event or activity.

Term	Description
Financial Framework	A set of high-level policies, procedures, and plans for coordinating, allocating, and managing funds.
Finish-to-Finish (FF)	In this logical relationship, the succeeding activity cannot be concluded until the preceding activity has finished. See also Finish-to-Start, Start-to-Finish, Start-to-Start, and Logical Relationship.
Finish-to-Start (FS)	In this logical relationship, the succeeding activity cannot be started until the preceding activity has finished. See also Finish-to-Finish, Start-to-Finish, Start-to-Start, and Logical Relationship.
Fit for Purpose	Suitability of a product for a particular use. For example, the ability of the customer to use the software for a particular purpose.
Fit for Use	Suitability of a product, in its present condition, for a particular use. For example, the ability of multiple customers to use the software simultaneously without significant performance deterioration.

Term	Description
Fixed Formula Method	An earned value scheme for the assignment of a portion of the budget value to the start milestone for a specific work package. It also has a remaining portion that is allocated once the work package is finished. See also Weighted Milestone Method.
Fixed Price (FP)	A contract type in which both the work and the fee are fixed. The negative risk is mainly held by the seller.
Fixed Price Incentive Fee Contract (FPIF)	A contract type in which both the work and the fee are fixed, but there can be an incentive for the seller should the work performance meet or exceed some pre-arranged parameters.
Fixed Price With Economic Price Adjustment Contracts (FP-EPA)	A contract type in which both the work and the fee are fixed, but there are special clauses in which the fee can be adjusted based on pre-determined changes external to the project.
Float	The duration of time for which a delay can be incurred by a task in the project network without delaying the completion date as well as subsequent tasks of the project. See also Free Float and Total Float.

Term	Description
Flow Master	A service request professional who acts as a part coach and part manager to ensure the smooth operation of a continuous flow of work or in a Kanban context. This role is equivalent to a Scrum Master in the Scrum methodology. Also see Scrum Master.
Focus Group	A group of knowledgeable people to predict future events based on information and available knowledge at the time of the forecast. In marketing, a focus group is used to evaluate the desirability of product features.
Forward Pass	A critical and essential scheduling path method for the determination of the early finish and early start dates for all the work segments, activities, or tasks that are uncompleted. Also see Backward Pass.
Framework	A structured approach supported by ideas, principles, facts, or a methodology.
Free Float	The duration for which a scheduled activity or task can undergo a delay without violation, in terms of a schedule constraint or an early start

Term	Description
	date of any succeeding schedule activity. See also Float and Total Float.
Functional Organization	A hierarchy in which areas of specialization form the basis of staff groupings. It also limits the authority of the project manager in terms of the application of resources and assignment of work. See also Matrix Organization and Projectized Organization.
Functional Requirement	A particular set of lower-level requirements that describes the behavior of a product, service, or application. In the Software Development Life Cycle (SDLC), functional requirements are developed from the business and stakeholder requirements. Also see Business Requirement and Functional Specification.
Functional Specification	A set of detailed documentation that describes the behavior of a product or service in conjunction with the planned technology to build the product or service. In the Software Development

Term	Description
	Life Cycle (SDLC), functional specifications are developed from the functional requirements and analyzed collectively within the technical environment in which the product or service will be built. Also see Functional Requirement.
Future State	The future state refers to a desired state that is often the intended outcome of projects, programs, and portfolios. Defining the future state is important to evaluate the effort required to progress from the current state to the desired future state. Also see Current State.
Future Value (FV)	The calculation of how much a present amount of money may be worth at some point in the future expressed as *Formula: Future Value = Present Value (1 + interest rate)n, where n is the number of time periods.* Also see Present Value (PV).

G

Term	Description
Gantt Chart	A bar chart that displays information regarding the project schedule where the horizontal axis represents dates, the vertical axis represents activities, and the horizontal bar shows the activity duration in accordance with their finish and start dates. Gantt charts can also show activity dependency relationships.
Goal	A general statement or description of the desired outcomes that an organization strives to achieve. Organizational goals are essential building blocks to achieving desired outcomes. Also see Objective.
Governance	The alignment of project, program, or portfolio goals with the sponsoring organization's strategy through sound decision-making processes on authorization, oversight, resource allocation, and change management. Also see Organizational Governance.

Term	Description
Governance Body	The governance board for the establishment of the project, program, and portfolio outline, activities, and processes for leading the activities and making key decisions. Also see Governance.
Governance Decision	A project, program, or portfolio decision made by steering committees or other governing bodies. The type of decision varies depending on the situation. An example includes course adjustment based on performance, component approvals, escalation of risks, and allocation of funds and investment resources.
Governance Framework	The management framework for making key decisions in project, program, or portfolio management. The framework should be logical, robust and repeatable to govern an organization's capital investments.
Governance Plan	A governance document outlining the actions and responsibilities to manage the project, program, or portfolio governance framework distilled from the Governance Strategy.

Term	Description
Governance Recommendation	A project, program, or portfolio recommendation made by steering committees or other governing bodies to organization leaders and executives. The type of recommendations varies depending on the situation. Examples include course adjustment based on performance, escalation of organizational risks, and allocation of major funds and investment resources.
Ground Rules	Basic rules and expectations for acceptable team behavior.
Guideline	Advice or recommendation that provides a procedure or an instruction on how something should be performed.

See Policy. |

H

Term	Description
Hoshin Kanri or Policy Deployment	A lean management method and technique of determining, developing, and disseminating policies to ensure alignment between actions and planning at every level within an organization. The goal is to eliminate waste that often comes from poor communication and direction setting.
Hybrid Approach	A framework based on multiple agile and non-agile components, typically resulting in a non-agile output that manifests some benefits of applying agile.

I

Term	Description
IDEAL (IDEAL)	An acronym for an organizational improvement model where the letters stand for Initiating, Diagnosing, Establishing, Acting, and Learning.
Impact Mapping	A strategic evaluation method that focuses on high impact scenarios on an organizational or product roadmap.
Impediment	A blocker that, unless removed or mitigated, will prevent the team from achieving its goals and objectives. Also see Blocker.
Increment	A useful, reliable, and acknowledged work. Typically, a subset of a larger endeavor.
Incremental Life Cycle	A type of life cycle in which the deliverables are built modularly such that each module is immediately usable or adds quantifiable value. Also see Agile Life Cycle, Iterative Life Cycle, Life Cycle, Predictive Life Cycle, and Product Life Cycle.

Term	Description
Information Management	A set of activities concerning information and the process to prepare, collect, organize, and secure it.
Information Management System (IMS)	A set of business processes, technology tools, and policy guidelines to manage the life cycle of information and knowledge, from the initial creation, through use and refinement, to eventual archive or termination. Often, this term has an additional descriptor in front of IMS, such as Project **P**IMS, Program **Pg**IMS, and Portfolio **Pf**IMS. Also see Project Management Information System (also Program and Portfolio Management Information System).
Information Radiator	A physical, easy-to-understand depiction of relevant project information that enables the immediate sharing of the information.
Initiative	A body of intended work that is loosely formed and has yet to solidify into concrete projects, programs, portfolios, or operational activities.

Term	Description
Integration Management	A collection of processes required to ensure that the various elements of the project, program, or portfolio are properly organized and coordinated.
Internal Rate of Return (IRR)	This is a financial metric used in financial analysis, such as investment justification. IRR is often used to compare the cost of capital for projects, programs, and portfolios. Also see Benefit-Cost Ratio, Net Present Value, and Payback Period.
Inventory of Work	A list of work that needs to be performed. For example, a list of active components to be implemented in a portfolio.
I-Shaped	The person having an in-depth knowledge or expertise in one area. Also see Broken Comb and T-Shape.
Issue	An occurring or occurred incident of a project or program that if unmanaged will affect the schedule, scope, cost, resources, or other project parameters. See also Opportunity, Risk, and Threat.

Term	Description
Iteration	A developmental cycle of a product in which all required activities are carried out within a pre-specified block of time.
Iterative Life Cycle	An approach to project implementation in which the finished product is built incrementally through multiple cycles. Each cycle should be of value to the customer. Also see Agile Life Cycle, Incremental Life Cycle, Life Cycle, Predictive Life Cycle, and Product Life Cycle.

K

Term	Description
Kaizen Event	Quality events focused on improving the overall product or system.
Kanban Board	A visualization tool that is often drawn on a board that illustrates the flow of work from inception to conclusion. The goal is to improve communication, transparency, and team empowerment by using an easy to read and highly accessible tool.
Kanban Method	An agile technique based on the philosophy that empowered knowledge workers would "pull" the work through the process from beginning to completion. This is opposed to the traditional approach of managers "pushing" work through the process.
Key Criteria	Values or measures applied in an evaluation activity to assess alignment between the target of evaluation with strategic goals.
Key Descriptor	A description of important characteristics used to provide clarity or richer details of the target subject to

Term	Description
	be used in the process of decision-making.
Key Performance Indicator (KPI)	A key measure as to how effective the performance of a project is in regards to agreed-upon, required, and identified strategic objectives. KPIs are often confused with Critical Success Factors (CSFs). Think of CSFs as "causes" for success, while KPIs are indicators that measure the "outputs" of striving toward that success. Also see Critical Success Factor (CSF).

L

Term	Description
Lag	The duration of time for which, in regards to a predecessor activity, a successor activity is delayed. Also see Lead.
Large Scale Scrum (LeSS)	A product development approach based on Scrum, which extends and scales Scrum for larger products.
Late Finish Date	The date that denotes the latest point at which the incomplete portions of a schedule activity or task may be concluded, without delaying the project completion date, while conforming to the scheduling constraints, on the basis of schedule network logic. Also see Early Finish Date, Early Start Date, Late Start Date, and Schedule Network Analysis.
Late Start Date	The date that denotes the latest point at which the incomplete portions of a scheduled activity may be started without delaying the project completion date, while conforming to

Term	Description
	the scheduling constraints, on the basis of schedule network logic. Also see Early Finish Date, Early Start Date, Late Finish Date, and Schedule Network Analysis.
Lead	The time duration in which a succeeding activity can be advanced in relation to the preceding activity. Also see Lag.
Lean Software Development (LSD)	An adaptation of the Lean management principles and activities toward software development. It is aimed at achieving better speed, higher quality, and greater client satisfaction.
Lessons Learned	Lessons learned is both an activity and a technique whereby a project, program, or portfolio is critically evaluated with the intent of understanding what worked well and identifying areas for future improvement. Prior to the start of a future initiative, a leading practice is to review the lessons learned knowledge base.

Term	Description
Level of Effort (LoF)	A support type of task or activity with no related outcomes or deliverables and is not on the critical path. Examples include the role of liaising, assorted project management activities, and some aspects of project cost accounting Also see Apportioned Effort and Discrete Effort.
Life Cycle	The process through which projects, programs, portfolios, and products are conceived, designed, implemented, and eventually terminated, from a beginning to an end. The Life Cycle is temporary by definition, even though some endeavors have significantly longer durations. Also see Agile Life Cycle, Incremental Life Cycle, Iterative Life Cycle, Predictive Life Cycle, and Product Life Cycle.

Term	Description
Logical Relationship	The existing reliance between two specific project elements (e.g. an activity and a milestone, or two activities). See also Finish-to-Finish, Finish-to-Start, Start-to-Finish, and Start-to-Start.

M

Term	Description
Make or Buy Decision	A determination of whether the project, program, or portfolio should develop and maintain a product or service internally or acquire it externally. Make or buy decisions are generally evaluated and made as a part of Supply Chain Management or Procurement Management.
Management Reserve	An active risk response strategy in which time or resources are proactively set aside to manage the unplanned or unknown project, program, or portfolio risks. Management reserves are generally held by the next level management and are financial in nature, but can extend to human, technical, and equipment resources. Also see Contingency Reserve, Project Budget, and Reserve.
Matrix Organization	An organizational framework in which responsibilities, including the application of resources and

Term	Description
	assignment of work, are shared by a program or project manager with a number of functional managers. See also Functional Organization and Projectized Organization.
Measure	A specific quantitative or qualitative unit for the evaluation of the degree, amount, or extent a project factor.
Metrics	A system of measures designed to evaluate the performance of an intended project dimension, such as schedule, cost, resources, or quality.
Milestone	A significant moment in time of a project, program, or portfolio, such as the completion of a major activity or phase.
Milestone Schedule	A form of schedule in which milestones are presented with their respective planned dates.
Minimal Viable Product (MVP)	This is an important concept from lean management and entrepreneurship that emphasizes developing products with the least effort in which customers are willing to pay. By learning from customer feedback that would translate to more frequent

Term	Description
	product releases, the product achieves an accelerated development cycle.
Mission	The statement of purpose of existence, or being, of the sponsoring organization (e.g. "Why do we exist?") Also see Vision.
Mobbing	A problem solving and work acceleration approach in which multiple team members coordinate their efforts and work simultaneously on a particular task or activity.
Model	An abstract and simple representation, generally created to enhance understanding in a given context.
Monte Carlo Simulation	A technique that simulates a target value (e.g. project cost or schedule) through many iterations to calculate a distribution of possible outcomes.

Term	Description
Most Likely Duration	An estimation of the most probable duration of a specific activity or task in which all known variables that may influence the performance of the whole program or project are taken into consideration. See also Optimistic Duration and Pessimistic Duration.

N

Term	Description
Near-Critical Activity	Based on expert judgment, an activity with a total float that is considered being low.
Near-Critical Path	An order of activities having a low float, becoming a critical path sequence if exhausted. Also see Critical Path.
Negotiation	The process of resolving disagreements or disputes among multiple parties, whereby compromise or agreement is reached thereby avoiding argument and dispute.
Net Present Value (NPV)	An economic measure that evaluates the present value of investments by considering the initiatives, investments, and returns across a series of time periods, often in years. Also see Benefit-Cost Ratio, Internal Rate of Return, and Payback Period.
Network Logic	The fundamental path that must be followed, depicting all the activity

Term	Description
	dependencies within a schedules network diagram.
Network Path	A continuous or consecutive series of projects or scheduled activities that may exhibit logical relationships as incorporated in the project network diagram.
Node	The connecting point for the dependency lines on the schedule network diagram.

O

Term	Description
Objective	The specific outcome in which work is directed such as a strategic position to be attained, a purpose to be achieved, a result to be obtained, a product to be produced, or a service to be performed. Favorable outcomes are the result of completing one or more goals successfully. Also see Goal.
Operation	The business function of managing the regular, often cyclical and routine activities of an organization.
Opportunity	A potential situation or condition that is favorable to one or multiple project objectives. See also Issue, Risk, and Threat.
Optimistic Duration	An estimation of the shortest activity duration that considers all the known variables that may have an impact on the performance.

Term	Description
	See also Most Likely Duration and Pessimistic Duration.
Organizational Bias	The implicit and often unspoken preference of an organization or team on a set of core values. For example, exploration of newness versus exploitation of existing capabilities; speed versus stability; quantity versus quality; flexibility versus discipline; and customer-centric versus operation-centric.
Organizational Breakdown Structure (OBS)	A tool utilized in a hierarchical manner for creating and conducting a clear and thoroughly delineated depiction of the relationships within and across the organizational units and work packages. Also see Resource Breakdown Structure, Risk Breakdown Structure, and Work Breakdown Structure (WBS).
Organizational Capabilities	The ability of an organization to leverage its people, processes, systems, and strategies to transform ideas, intended goals, and objectives into tangible results and outcomes. Also see Goals and objective

Term	Description
Organizational Change Management (OCM)	An organizational approach to transforming organizations or teams or shifting individuals mindsets and behaviors from the current state to the desired future state.
Organizational Enabler	A cultural, structural, human, finance, or technological practice that can be utilized by the performing organization in order to accomplish an organization's strategic goals and objectives.
Organizational Governance	An organization's control over its strategy, operations, and activities. Also see Governance.
Organizational Process Assets (OPA)	Processes, plans, knowledge, procedures, and policies utilized by and pertinent to, the performing organization (e.g. formal and informal plans, policies, procedures, and guidelines). Also see Process Asset (Project, Program, and Portfolio).

Term	Description
Organizational Project Management (OPM)	A structure in which project, program, and portfolio management are incorporated with organizational enablers for accomplishing strategic goals and objectives. Also see Goals and Objectives
Organizational Project Management Maturity (OPMM)	The capability of an organization in terms of delivering the intended strategic goals and objectives in a reliable, controllable, and predictable manner.
Organizational Strategy and Objectives	An official document comprising the organization's vision and mission statements and its strategic goals and objectives. Also see Goals and Objectives.
Output	The immediate result of a project, either individually or collectively, as part of an organization's project activities and tasks. This term is often confused with "outcome", which is the longer-term consequence of how a project turns out.

P

Term	Description
Paint-Drip	See Broken Comb.
Pair Programming	An agile software development technique in which two or more programmers work together at one workstation. The main driver creates codes while the other(s) observe, navigate, suggest, and check for quality as the driver writes the codes.
Pair Work	A technique focused on quality and accelerated development, where two team members are paired to work together simultaneously on the same work. This way, one person can check and validate the work of another person. In agile software development, this is known as Pair Programming.
Pairing	See Pair Work.
Parametric Estimating	An estimation scheme involving an algorithm for calculating duration or cost on the basis of project or program parameters and historical data. Also see Analogous Estimating, Bottom-up Estimating, Definitive

Term	Description
	Estimating, Program Evaluation and Review Technique (PERT), and Three-Point Estimating.
Pareto Diagram	A diagram, represented by a histogram, showing the frequency of occurrence identifying how many outcomes were produced as a result of each cause.
Pareto Principle	This is a statistical principle which states that 80 percent of a target effect is derived from 20 percent of sources or causes for a particular event or activity. For example, 80% of project challenges come from 20% of the sources. Also see 80/20 Rule.
Parkinson's Law	A general law that describes a phenomenon in which work somehow expands to fill the allotted amount of time.
Path Convergence	A relationship having more than one predecessor associated with a schedule activity. See also Path Divergence, Predecessor Activity, and Successor Activity.

Term	Description
Path Divergence	A relationship having more than one successor associated with a schedule activity. See also Path Divergence, Predecessor Activity, and Successor Activity.
Payback Period	An economic analysis that refers to the amount of time it takes to break even or to recuperate the cost of investment. A shorter payback period is more financially more attractive. Also see Benefit-Cost Ratio, Internal Rate of Return, and Net Present Value.
PDSA Cycle (or Model)	This is a continuous improvement process of **P**lan, **D**o, **S**tudy, and **A**ct. The goal is to evaluate and implement a change through rapid planning, doing the work, observing and studying the consequences, and acting to or perfect the change.
Percent Complete	An estimation stated as a portion of the work amount, which has been finished on a work breakdown structure component or an activity.

Term	Description
	Also see Work Breakdown Structure.
Performance Measurement Baseline	Integrated cost, schedule, and scope baselines utilized to compare for controlling, measuring, and managing project execution.

Also see Baseline, Cost Baseline, Schedule Baseline, and Scope Baseline. |
| Performing Organization | A particular group or enterprise that is explicitly and directly involved in all aspects and phases of doing any and all work of the respective project. This term is also referred to as the "Sponsoring Organization".

See also Sponsoring Organization. |
| Persona | An archetype user characterizing a group of same end users delineated with their objectives, goals, and individual characteristic properties. |
| Pessimistic Duration | An estimation of the longest activity duration that considers every known parameter with which performance could be influenced. |

Term	Description
	See also Most Likely Duration and Optimistic Duration.
Phase	A group of related activities that collectively culminate in the completion of one or multiple deliverables.
Phase Gate	A project, program, or portfolio management activity that objectively assesses and evaluates the end of the initiatives phase. The Phase Gate is important for making decisions related to continuing to the successive phase, for ending the endeavor, or for continuing with modification.
Phase Gate Review	A decision process that evaluates and reevaluates a project or program at a pre-determined point and determines whether the initiative should move forward to the next successive phase.
Pivot	A deliberate and planned course correction designed to evaluate a new theory about the product or strategy.
Plan-Do-Check-Act (PDCA)	A continuous improvement framework, which provides a simple and effective approach for managing change and solving problems. The framework can also be applied to iterative product

Term	Description
	development, to incremental project management, and for testing improvement measures on a small scale before deploying to a broader context. Also known as the Deming Cycle.
Plan-Driven Approach	See Predictive Approach.
Planned Value (PV)	An element of Earned Value Management, PV refers to the authorized budget allocated for scheduled work. Planned Value is calculated by multiplying the planned percentage of the completed work by the project budget. Also see Actual Cost (AC), Budget at Completion (BAC), Earned Value (EV), Estimate at Completion (EAC), and Estimate to Complete (ETC).
Plurality	A decision-making concept in which the term refers to the largest block of people with a similar choice.
Policy	A structured and deliberate set of organizational rules and instructions that provide basic principles to guide an organization's conduct.

Term	Description
	Also see Guideline.
Portfolio	A logical collection of programs, projects, operations, subsidiary portfolios, and other related work that should be managed collectively to achieve one or more of organizational and strategic goals and objectives.
Portfolio Balancing	The optimization and sequencing of portfolio components to enhance the strategic goals and objectives of the organization.
Portfolio Management (PfM)	The centralized streamlining of one or multiple portfolios for the achievement of strategic goals and objectives by incorporating the concepts of identifying, prioritizing, authorizing, monitoring, and controlling of the entirety of the portfolio.
Portfolio Management Office (PfMO)	A management structure responsible for the centralized management and coordination of portfolio(s) within the organization. Note: The general acronym is PMO. This dictionary is using PfMO to differentiate Project Management Office (PMO), Program Management

Term	Description
	Office (PgMO), and Enterprise Project Management Office (EPMO). Also see Enterprise Project Management Office, Project Management Office, and Program Management Office.
Portfolio Management Plan	A document stating the specifications of the portfolio in terms of controlling, monitoring, and organizing a portfolio.
Portfolio Management Professional (PfMP®)	Project Management Institute's professional-level certification for portfolio managers. This certification is currently the apex of the project management professional ladder, especially with an emphasis on business and governance processes. Attaining this certification is a demonstration of leadership, organizational savviness, and business acumen to make business investment decisions and lead their implementation.
Portfolio Manager	An individual that a performing organization assigns for balancing, establishing, controlling, and monitoring portfolio components for the achievement of strategic business

Term	Description
	goals and objectives. Also see Project Manager and Program Manager.
Portfolio Optimization	The ongoing process of balancing and rebalancing the portfolio to optimize the use of resources, balance risk with rewards, and adjust for risk and changes.
Practice	The actual application or use of an idea, belief, or method that may employ one or more techniques and tools to achieve a specific goal.
Precedence Diagraming Method (PDM)	A scheme utilized for designing a schedule model in which nodes that represent activities are also associated graphically by one or multiple logical relationships for exhibiting the series in which activities must be carried out.
Precision	The measure of exactness. Measurements that are close to each other are said to be precise. Also see Accuracy.
Predecessor Activity	A work schedule activity in a program or project that establishes or determines when an activity can

Term	Description
	logically supersede a dependent activity. See also Path Convergence, Path Divergence, Successor Activity, and Work Breakdown Structure.
Predictive Approach	A framework of performing work based on the deliberate and detailed planning of the work typically applied through the life cycle of a project, program, or portfolio.
Predictive Life Cycle	A type of project life cycle that is deliberately planned in detail at every stage before sequentially progressing toward the next stage of development. As compared with an adaptive or agile life cycle, a predictive life cycle is often viewed as a "traditional life cycle". Also see Agile Life Cycle, Incremental Life Cycle, Iterative Life Cycle, Predictive Life Cycle, and Product Life Cycle.
Present Value (PV)	Defines what a future amount of money is worth today. The formula is: *Formula: Present Value = Future Value/(1 + interest rate)n,*

Term	Description
	where n represents the time periods. Also see Future Value (FV).
Preventive Action	An intentional activity that ensures the alignment between the project management plan and project work's future performance. Also see Corrective Action.
Probability and Impact Matrix	A two-by-two matrix for mapping the probability of risk occurrence and its impact on project or program objectives if that risk occurs. See also Risk.
Procedure	A series of actions conducted in a certain order or manner to achieve a required goal or outcome.
Process	A series of deliberate actions or steps taken in order to achieve a particular outcome or output.
Process Asset (PPA)	Strategies, policies, processes, and data of the project, program, or portfolio used by the stakeholders and managers. Also see Organizational Process Assets.

Term	Description
Procurement Management	The practice of identifying, evaluating, and managing supply chain processes through the application of knowledge, skills, and tools required for the effective and efficient implementation of a project, program, and portfolio.
Procurement Management Plan	A plan in which the entirety of the procurement process is described, which expounds the process as to how services and goods will be acquired that may be outside of the enterprise. According to the *PMBOK® Guide*, this is a component plan within the Project Management Plan.
Product	A result, outcome, or artifact at the successful completion of a project or program.
Product Backlog	Commonly used in agile, it contains a listing of all activities, tasks, new features, changes to existing features, or bug fixes, which need to be completed to fulfill project or product requirements satisfactorily or to achieve a specific outcome.
Product Life Cycle	The range of principally sequential product phases in terms of their evolution, usually completely non-

Term	Description
	overlapping, from conception to maturity, growth, delivery, and retirement. Also see Agile Life Cycle, Incremental Life Cycle, Iterative Life Cycle, Life Cycle, and Predictive Life Cycle.
Product Owner	A member of the agile team responsible for maximizing the value of the product, team, and the Scrum approach by defining user stories and prioritizing the product backlog to streamline the execution of project priorities.
Professional in Business Analysis (PMI-PBA®) (PMI-PBA®)	Project Management Institute's professional-level certification for project business analysts who specialize in the development of project and product scope and requirements.
Program	A collection of highly related components, such as sub-programs, projects, and other activities. When these components are managed as a program, they can achieve great value and benefits not possible if they were managed separately.

Term	Description
Program Charter	Issued by the Sponsor, this document authorizes the program team to utilize organizational resources for the execution of the initiative. The Program Charter also connects the strategic goals and objectives of the organization with the program.
Program Evaluation and Review Technique (PERT)	A method in which a weighted average of pessimistic, optimistic, and most likely activity durations is taken into consideration for the estimation of project duration when the individual estimates involve uncertainty. Also see Analogous Estimating, Bottom-up Estimating, Definitive Estimating, Parametric Estimating, and Three-Point Estimating.
Program Management (PgM)	The coordinated management of program activities by applying specific principles, knowledge, processes, tools, and skills to deliver results effectively.
Program Management Office (PgMO)	A management framework in which the program-related governance processes are standardized, and also assists in the sharing process of methodologies, resources, techniques, and tools.

Term	Description
	Note: The general acronym is PMO. This dictionary is using PgMO to differentiate Project Management Office (PMO), Portfolio Management Office (PfMO), and Enterprise Project Management Office (EPMO) Also see Enterprise Project Management Office, Project Management Office, and Portfolio Management Office.
Program Management Plan	A document that provides for the establishment of the overall plan and controls for management and integration of the individual components of the program, as well as the integration of subsidiary plans of the program.
Program Management Professional (PgMP®)	Project Management Institute's professional-level certification for program managers. Achieving this certification indicates the professional's competency at leading a group of related projects and activities and to achieve greater value than managing these components individually.

Term	Description
Program Manager	The authorized individual by the performing enterprise for the purpose of leading the team or teams that work for the achievement of program goals. Also see Project Manager and Portfolio Manager.
Progressive Elaboration	A method in which the plan for the designated and particular project is being constantly and continuously improved, detailed, and modified as more accurate information becomes available.
Project	A time-limited, purpose-driven, and often unique endeavor intended to create an outcome, service, product, or deliverable.
Project Calendar	A calendar in which the project is delineated and/or outlined in terms of working shifts and days against the scheduled activities.
Project Charter	A document issued by an individual or group responsible for sponsoring or initiating the project. The project charter grants formal authorization to the project manager to guide and oversee activities within the context of

Term	Description
	organizational, contractual, and third-party resources.
Project Expeditor	A project management role in which a person supports the project manager or project executive by administering the agreed upon project management processes and tools.
Project Management	A management discipline specialized for overseeing projects. Project management includes the activities associated with initiating, planning, executing, monitoring, controlling, and closing the work for meeting the project goals and objectives by applying skills, knowledge, techniques, and tools to project activities and tasks.
Project Management Information System (also Program and Portfolio Management Information System) (PMIS)	A management method for collecting, integrating, imaging, preserving, distributing, and terminating the knowledge and information created in the implementation of a project, program, or portfolio.

Term	Description
Project Management Office (PMO)	A management framework that assists in the sharing of methodologies, leading practices, resources, techniques, and tools as well as the standardization of the governance processes that are related to the project. Note: The general acronym PMO can represent Project-, Program-, and Portfolio Management Office. This dictionary makes the distinction and correspondingly, the acronym used is PMO, PgMO, and PfMO (project, program, and portfolio respectively.) Also see Enterprise Project Management Office, Program Management Office, and Portfolio Management Office.
Project Management Plan	A comprehensive planning document, or collection of documents, that describes how a project will be planned, implemented, monitored, controlled, and closed.

Term	Description
Project Management Professional (PMP®)	Project Management Institute's professional-level certification for project managers. This certification is designed to cement a working knowledge of project management and the leadership competencies to direct projects.
Project Manager	A project leadership role, authorized by the performing organization, to apply the resources, direct the project team, and manage the project activities to achieve the intended goals and objectives. Also see Program Manager and Portfolio Manager.
Project Schedule Network Diagram	An output/input graphical illustration that represents logical relationships that may exist between the project schedule activities.
Projectification	A social phenomenon in which activities and work are viewed through the lens of projects. What constitutes projects can be complicated, but projects usually exhibit these features: time-bound, goal-oriented, constraints, and uniqueness. The uniqueness can appear in one or more areas, such as

Term	Description
	unique outcome, environmental context, or stakeholder involvement.
Projectized Organization	An organizational framework in which ultimate authority is assigned to the program or project manager in terms of making any or all decisions including the application of resources, and the assignment of all priorities. See also Functional Organization and Matrix Organization.
PRojects IN Controlled Environments (PRINCE2)	This is a structured project management method largely adopted in Europe (the UK, Western European nations, and Australia). PRINCE2 is also the name of a project management certification supported by AXELOS.

Q

Term	Description
Quality	The extent to which a set of attributes produced by projects and programs meet the stakeholder, business, functional, non-functional, and transition requirements.
Quality Assurance (QA)	Project, program, and portfolio activities associated with preventing mistakes and defects, and avoiding problems when delivering the endeavor to customers. Quality Assurance (QA) focuses on getting ahead of defects. Also see Cost of Quality, Quality Planning, and Quality Control.
Quality Audits	A process to assess a level of conformance or non-conformance to requirements of a system, process, product, or technology.
Quality Checklists	A tool used to aid the project team in ensuring they consider all aspects of the project and/or process quality.

Term	Description
Quality Control	Project, program, and portfolio activities intended to ensure that a manufactured program adheres to a defined set of quality criteria or meets the requirements of the client or customer. Quality Control (QC) focuses on identifying and fixing defects after they occur. Also see Cost of Quality, Quality Planning, and Quality Assurance.
Quality Management	The process for ensuring that all project and program activities necessary to design, plan, and implement an initiative are effective and efficient with respect to the purpose of the objective and its performance.
Quality Management Plan	A plan that expounds the exact methodology, guidelines, procedures, and policies that would be implemented by the organization in order to accomplish the quality targets. According to the *PMBOK® Guide*, this is a component plan within the project management plan.

Term	Description
Quick Win	A quick win is an improvement or value-add that can be achieved quickly after projects, programs, or portfolios start. The goal of quick wins is to build positive momentum for change.

R

Term	Description
RACI / Responsibility Assignment Matrix (RAM)	A specific type of Responsibility Assignment Matrix (RAM) that is also an acronym where R stands for **R**esponsibility, A for **A**ccountability, C for **C**onsulted, and I for **I**nformed.
Refactoring	A quality technique in which the product designed is improved, either in usability or maintainability, without changing the expected behavior of the product.
Regression Analysis	A statistical technique that involves examining the series of input variables in relation to the corresponding output results. It is used in establishing the statistical relationship between two variables.
Request for Information (RFI)	A procurement process and the associated document whereby the buyer requests various information on a product or service from potential sellers, typically without a commitment to purchase. In most situations, the Request for Information (RFI) occurs very early in the procurement process where the buyer and seller may even

Term	Description
	meet for the first time. Also see Request for Proposal (RFP) and Request for Quotation (RFQ).
Request for Proposal (RFP)	A procurement process and the associated document whereby the buyer requests specific information and pricing on a product or service from prospective sellers. Typically, the Request for Proposal (RFP) occurs later in the procurement process where mutual interests are already determined, often following the Request for Information (RFI) and Request for Quotation (RFQ) process. In some instances, this process and document can be formal. Also see Request for Information (RFI) and Request for Quotation (RFQ).
Request for Quotation (RFQ)	A procurement process and the associated document whereby the buyer requests specific indicative or approximate pricing on a product or service from prospective sellers. Typically, the Request for Quote (RFQ) follows the Request for Information (RFI) process.

Term	Description
	Also see Request for Information (RFI) and Request for Proposal (RFP).
Requirement	A condition or capability that is required to be present in a product, service, or result to satisfy a contract or other formally imposed requirement. Commonly categorized as stakeholder, business, functional, non-functional, and transition.
Requirements Management Plan	A constituent of the project management plan that explicitly identifies the method and process for which the requirements will be identified, documented, analyzed, managed, and controlled over the duration of the project. Also see Business Requirement and Functional Requirement.
Requirements Traceability Matrix	A matrix that connects the origin of the requirements to the associated deliverables and traces the identified items to an organization's goals, objectives, and underlying Business Case which was used to Charter the initiative.
Reserve	Financial and non-financial resources held by the Governance team to address the project, program, and

Term	Description
	portfolio risks. Also see Contingency Reserve and Management Reserve.
Residual Risk	The risk that remains after risk assessments and the implementation of their respective responses.
Resistance Mitigation	Methods or techniques to reduce change resistance such as communication, training, and stakeholder engagement. The goal of resistance mitigation is to improve organization adoption and acceptance of organizational change. Also see Change Fatigue and Change Resistance.
Resource Breakdown Structure (RBS)	A hierarchal model that logically presents the project, program, or portfolio resources in an organized manner, often by types and categories. Also see Organizational Breakdown Structure, Risk Breakdown Structure, and Work Breakdown Structure (WBS).
Resource Calendar	A calendar that lists all the nonworking, as well as the working days that may be utilized for determining the dates for

Term	Description
	which a specific resource is engaged, utilized, or available.
Resource Leveling	A technique for resource optimization to adjust hours available for work per team member, and the number of hours allocated to each individual, which may influence the critical path. Also see Resource Optimization Technique and Resource Smoothing.
Resource Management	The practice of identifying, evaluating, and managing human and non-human resources required for the successful planning and implementation of a project, program, and portfolio.
Resource Management Plan	A comprehensive plan utilized for allocation and acquisition planning, implementing, monitoring, controlling, and closing of project resources. According to the PMBOK® Guide, this is a component plan within the Project Management Plan.
Resource Optimization Technique	A technique to optimize project, program, and portfolio schedules and resources by redistributing and balancing supply and demand.

Term	Description
	Also see Resource Leveling and Resource Smoothing.
Resource Smoothing	A technique for adjusting the schedule model activities by using the total and free float so all resource requirements stay within the resource limitations while conforming to the critical path. Also see Resource Leveling and Resource Optimization Technique.
Responsibility Assignment Matrix (RAM)	A table that describes a project or program resource assignments on tasks, activities, deliverables, or work packages. Also see RACI / Responsibility Assignment Matrix.
Retrospective	A regular meeting of the project team, generally taking place after the completion of an iteration or sprint, with the intention of improving future iterations.
Risk	A potentiality that, if it materializes, can have an impact on one or multiple objectives negatively or positively, in the form of resources, performance, quality, or timeline.

Term	Description
	See also Issue, Opportunity, Probability and Impact Matrix, and Threat.
Risk Acceptance	A risk response strategy in which the portfolio, program, or project team agrees not to alter the management plan for dealing with the risk unless it is incurred. Also see Risk Avoidance, Risk Enhancement, Risk Exploiting, Risk Mitigation, Risk Sharing, and Risk Transference.
Risk Appetite	The level of uncertainty a stakeholder or organization is willing to tolerate in anticipation of attaining rewards. Also see Risk Threshold and Risk Tolerance.
Risk Avoidance	A threat or negative risk response strategy in which the portfolio, program, or project team agrees to eliminate the threat by evading the risk completely. Also see Risk Acceptance, Risk Enhancement, Risk Exploiting, Risk Mitigation, Risk Sharing, and Risk Transference.

Term	Description
Risk Breakdown Structure	A hierarchically organized representation of risks as well as their potential sources. Also see Organizational Breakdown Structure, Resource Breakdown Structure, and Work Breakdown Structure (WBS).
Risk Category	A set of risks and their potential causes with respect to their categories.
Risk Enhancement	An opportunity or positive risk response strategy in which the portfolio, program, or project team acts to increase the probability of the risk occurrence or impact should the risk occur. Also see Risk Avoidance, Risk Acceptance, Risk Exploiting, Risk Mitigation, Risk Sharing, and Risk Transference.
Risk Exploiting	An opportunity or positive risk response strategy in which the portfolio, program, or project team acts to ensure the risk will occur. Also see Risk Avoidance, Risk Acceptance, Risk Enhancement, Risk

Term	Description
	Mitigation, Risk Sharing, and Risk Transference.
Risk Exposure	An aggregation of all the quantifiable potential impacts of all risks at any time in a portfolio, program, or project.
Risk Management	The practice of identifying, evaluating, prioritizing, and monitoring unknown and probable events that may affect projects, programs, and portfolios. Once prioritized, selective risks are analyzed further to develop a risk response plan and when necessary implement them to mitigate threats and exploit opportunities.
Risk Management Plan	A portfolio, program, or project management deliverable or artifact that outlines the risk management procedures and activities that will be performed in terms of its performance and structure.

According to the *PMBOK® Guide*, this is a component plan within the Project Management Plan. |
| Risk Management Professional (PMI-RMP®) | Project Management Institute's professional-level certification for project managers who specialize in risk management. This certification is designed to indicate the individual's |

Term	Description
	risk management competency including the application of project risk management concepts, processes, tools, and techniques.
Risk Mitigation	A technique for risk response in which measures are taken by a portfolio, program, or project manager to reduce or eliminate the occurrence probability of risks and impacts.
Risk Owner	An individual who is entrusted with the responsibility to monitor the risks and execute strategies for risk responses.
Risk Register	A repository that captures the essential details of the project, program, and portfolio risks.
Risk Sharing	An opportunity or positive risk response strategy in which the portfolio, program, or project team distributes or allocates the risk ownership to another party for the purpose of maximizing the benefits. Also see Risk Avoidance, Risk Acceptance, Risk Exploiting, Risk Enhancement, Risk Mitigation, and Risk Transference.
Risk Threshold	The maximum amount or volume of uncertainty around an objective that a

Term	Description
	stakeholder or organization is willing to accept. The concept of risk threshold is closely associated with risk appetite. Also see Risk Appetite and Risk Tolerance
Risk Tolerance	The amount, volume, or degree of risk that an enterprise can willingly endure. Also see Risk Threshold and Risk Tolerance.
Risk Transference	A threat or negative risk response strategy in which the portfolio, program, or project team shifts the impact of a risk to a third party, sometimes including the ownership of the response. Also see Risk Acceptance, Risk Avoidance, Risk Enhancement, Risk Exploiting, Risk Mitigation, Risk Sharing, and Risk Transference.
Roadmap (Program and Portfolio)	A visual map that illustrates how the program or portfolio components are linked together and work toward achieving the strategic goals of an organization.

Term	Description
Rolling Wave Planning	An iterative technique that involves progressive elaboration for adding details to the work that has to be completed in the near-term on an ongoing basis, while a higher level for planning is used for work that has to be done in the future.

S

Term	Description
Scaled Agile Framework (SAFe®)	A set of integrated workflow and patterns intended to guide lean and agile practices and scale them for enterprises.
Schedule	An output of a schedule model that keeps track of any or all planned dates for the linked activities and predetermined dates that are anticipated to be adhered to in terms of achieving project or program milestones.
Schedule Baseline	The approved schedule model version that is utilized as a reference for comparing with the actual results for determining if a preventive action, corrective action, or change is required. Also see Baseline, Cost Baseline, Performance Measurement Baseline, and Scope Baseline.
Schedule Compression	An approach to project scheduling, whereby the duration is shortened, while not minimizing and/or reducing the scope or quality of the project in

Term	Description
	any way. See also Crashing and Fast Tracking.
Schedule Management	A project management work effort that identifies and establishes the sequencing and timing of project activities in order to develop the project, program, or portfolio schedule, identify milestones, enable tracking of progress, and document planned accomplishments. Collectively the goal is to produce the intended deliverables, benefits, and value.
Schedule Management Plan	The document that defines the criteria for maintaining and developing the actual schedule of the initiative, which is included as a subsidiary of the management plan of the program or project. According to the PMBOK® Guide, this is a component plan within the Project Management Plan.
Schedule Model	A tool for creating the overall project schedule by taking into consideration a representation for the execution of activities of the project including planning information, dependencies, and durations.

Term	Description
	Also see Schedule Model Analysis.
Schedule Model Analysis	A process for analyzing the schedule model with the intention of optimizing the schedule. Also see Schedule Model.
Schedule Network Analysis	A technique for generating the project management schedule, by considering the late and early start dates, for the segments of the project activities that are incomplete. Also see Early Finish Date, Early Start Date, Late Start Date, and Late Finish Date.
Schedule Performance Index (SPI)	Earned Value Management measures designed to evaluate project or program schedule efficiency. It is expressed as a ratio of Earned Value (EV) to Planned Value (PV). *Formula: SPI = EV / PV* Also see Cost Performance Index (CPI).
Schedule Variance (SV)	A quantitative measure for determining schedule performance after or during the project completion, expressed when Planned Value (PV) is subtracted

Term	Description
	from the Earned Value (EV). *Formula: SV = EV - PV.* Also see Cost Variance (CV).
Scheduling Professional (PMI-SP®)	Project Management Institute's professional-level certification for project scheduler who specializes in project scheduling methods and the ability to manage time. This certification is designed to indicate the individual's ability to manage schedules of large and often complex projects.
Scope	The sum of the products, services, and results to be provided as a project, program, or portfolio.
Scope Baseline	The approved version of Work Breakdown Structure, scope statement, and the WBS dictionary that serves as a formal point of reference with respect to the agreed project scope. By utilizing formal procedures for change control, the scope baseline can be altered. Also see Baseline, Cost Baseline, Performance Measurement Baseline, and Schedule Baseline.

Term	Description
Scope Creep	An expansion to the program, project, or product scope in an unrestrained manner without regard to resources, quality, cost, and/or time.
Scope Management	A deliberate activity that identifies, defines, develops, tracks, controls, and validates the agreed upon work to fulfill the requirements of a project, program, or portfolio.
Scope Management Plan	A component of the program or project management plan that explicates the mechanism for which the scope will be defined, developed, verified, controlled, and monitored. According to the *PMBOK® Guide*, this is a component plan within the Project Management Plan.
Scope Statement	The description of the project, program, or portfolio scope that includes objectives, assumptions, deliverables, and constraints.
Scrum	A popular agile project management framework that emphasizes daily communication, flexible assessment of work, short and timeboxed development and deployment cycles, and multiple iterations (called sprints).

Term	Description
Scrum Board	An illustrative tool that displays the product and sprint backlog and shows a visual representation of the flow of activities and any obstacles and bottlenecks.
Scrum Master	A project role in which a professional serves as a part coach and part facilitator to manage the flow of work activities in a Scrum sprint. The roles include facilitating prioritization and problem solving, removing obstacles, and protecting the team resources from disruptions and external interventions. Also see Flow Master.
Scrum of Scrums	A mechanism to scale up the Scrum method for multiple teams working collectively on the same product or towards the same higher-order objectives. This is likely in a virtual team environment composed of representatives from the related Scrum teams. This "super-team" works collectively to ensure the synchronization of developmental goals, integration of necessary parts, resolving common challenges, and

Term	Description
	collaborating frequently to achieve the product goals.
Scrum Team	Typically a small team composed of a Scrum Master, Product Owner, and team members often cross-trained with multiple skills.
Scrumban	An agile development methodology that is a hybrid of Scrum and Kanban. Scrumban emerged to meet the needs of teams wanting to minimize the batching of work and the adoption of a pull-based system.
S-Curve Analysis	A tool that uses a graphical display of cumulative costs over a particular duration of time for the indication of performance trends.
Secondary Risk	A risk generated as a consequence of implementing a risk response scheme for another risk.
Self-Organizing Team	A cross-functional team in which people choose how best to accomplish their work by choosing their own leadership rather than being directed by others outside the team.
Sensitivity Analysis	An assessment of the degree of impact that a change would incur on project, program, or portfolio results.

Term	Description
Servant Leadership	A philosophy and a set of practices that enriches the lives of individuals, builds better organizations, and ultimately creates a more just and caring world. Servant Leadership is often associated with agile as the preferred leadership style.
Service Request Manager	The person who is responsible for handling customer requests and managing the customer relationship from the time of the request to delivery.
Severity	The degree to which a defect impacts the operability and performance of a software or product.
Siloed Organization	A type of organizational structure in which various business units, such as departments or product teams, are focused exclusively or almost exclusively, on its goals and often without collaboration with other business units. For contrast, see Value Stream.
Single Loop Learning	A learning process that analyzes the results of a process and determines ways of improvement.

Term	Description
	Also see Double Loop Learning.
Smoke Testing	A type of software testing that comprises a non-exhaustive set of tests that aim to ensure that the most important functions work. The results of this testing are used to decide if a build is stable enough to proceed with further testing.
Specification	A document outlining all goals, functionality, and details required for a development team to fulfill the vision of the client.
Specification by Example	A collaborative approach to defining business-oriented functional requirements and test scenarios for software products, based on capturing and demonstrating requirements with realistic examples and use cases rather than abstract statements.
Spike	An escalation in project resources, typically for a short period, to address a particular problem effectively, conduct research, or to build a prototype.
Sponsor	An accountable individual for enabling success who is also responsible for providing support and resources for

Term	Description
	the portfolio, program, or project. The person(s) is responsible for issuing the Charter.
Sponsoring Organization	A particular group or enterprise that is explicitly and directly involved in the funding and execution of the project, program, or portfolio. This term is also referred to as the "performing organization". See also Performing Organization.
Sprint	A timeboxed iteration in Scrum in which the resources are also sometimes fixed.
Sprint Backlog	A list of tasks identified by the Scrum team to be completed during the Scrum sprint.
Sprint Planning	A collaborative effort involving a Scrum Master, who facilitates the meeting; a Product Owner, who clarifies the details of the product backlog items and their respective acceptance criteria; and the entire agile Team, who define the work and effort necessary to meet their sprint commitment.
Staffing Management Plan	A document that explicates the various requirements for human resources that will be met for both employees and

Term	Description
	staff, including management, along with the acquiring process and duration of the acquirement of the team members.
Stakeholder	An organization, group, or individual that has the capacity to influence, be affected by, or consider itself under the influence of, an outcome, activity, or decision of a portfolio, program, or project.
Stakeholder Analysis	The process and technique of assessing expectations of an individual or a group of individuals who are interested or influenced by the project, program, or portfolio.
Stakeholder Engagement	The process of managing people's expectations who may be affected or influenced by a project, program, or portfolio.
Stakeholder Engagement Plan	A component of the project, program, or portfolio management plan that is used for identifying the actions and strategies needed for the promotion of constructive identification, categorization, and engagement of stakeholders in project, program, or portfolio execution and decision-making.

Term	Description
Standard Deviation (SD)	Standard deviation is a statistical measure of data disbursement. This can be used to measure a variety of phenomena on projects, programs, and portfolios such as stakeholder sentiment, estimation accuracy, and margin of errors on factors such as quality and risk analysis.
Start-to-Finish (SF)	A logical relationship that defines the sequence in which a succeeding activity cannot be completed unless a preceding activity has finished. See also Finish-to-Start, Finish-to-Finish, Start-to-Start, and Logical Relationship.
Start-to-Start (SS)	A logical relationship that defines the sequence in which a succeeding activity cannot be started unless a preceding activity has finished. See also Finish-to-Start, Finish-to-Finish, Start-to-Finish, and Logical Relationship.
Steering Committee (SC)	The governance board responsible for important decision-making such as oversight, change management, and approval of the project, program, portfolio, and/or their components.

Term	Description
Story Point	A metric used to determine or estimate the amount of work required to implementing a user story.
Strategic Alignment	The process of linking and evaluating organizational strategy with project, program, and portfolio goals and objectives, taking into account the business environment and any implementation challenges.
Strategic Business Execution (SBE)	An interdisciplinary framework to deliver consistent and sustainable business results through focus and prioritization, close alignment between strategy and implementation, thoughtful planning, disciplined execution, and sensible agility to manage changes and unknowns.
Strategic Change	A restructuring of an organization's business that is typically performed in response to internal or environmental changes and to achieve important objectives.
Strategic Initiative	An endeavor intended to achieve the lasting value of an organization.
Strategic Objective	The measurable long-term or lasting goals and intentions (e.g. economic, customers, innovations), products and

Term	Description
	services, and supporting technology and infrastructure.
Strategic Plan	A formal plan that bridges the gap between strategy and implementation and ensures that an organization can leverage its portfolio, program, and project selection, and execution processes.
Strategic Planning	An organization's process of defining its strategy or direction and making decisions on allocating its resources to pursue its strategy. It may also extend to reporting and control mechanisms for guiding the implementation of the strategy.
Strategy Alignment	Project, program, and portfolio management activities responsible for linking and integrating the organizational strategy with the project, program, and portfolio strategy and practices.
Strategy Implementation	A procedure of putting strategies and plans into action for achieving the desired business objectives. It can be in the form of a written document that states the processes and steps required for reaching goals of the plan and also

Term	Description
	includes progress and feedback reports for ensuring effective progress.
Successor Activity	A dependent activity that occurs following a predecessor activity in a schedule. See also Path Convergence, Path Divergence, Predecessor Activity, and Successor Activity.
Summary Activity	A single activity that is an accumulation of a group of related activities. Also see Predecessor Activity and Successor Activity.
Supply and Demand Allocation	The effective allocation of organizational resources to meet the demand from a project, program, and portfolio. Supply and Demand is a major concept in the Standard for Portfolio Management Third Edition.
Supply and Demand Analysis	The analysis of organizational resources to balance the supply of organizational resources with the demand of those from a project, program, and portfolio. Supply and Demand is a major concept

Term	Description
	in the Standard for Portfolio Management Third Edition.
Supply and Demand Management	The management of organizational resources to balance the need for resources (demand) against the available organizational resources (supply).
	Supply and Demand is a major concept in the Standard for Portfolio Management Third Edition.
Swarming	A technique in which a group comes together for a short-term project to overcome a particular impediment and quickly disbands when the problem has been resolved.
SWOT Analysis (SWOT)	A strategic planning tool used to evaluate an organization's **S**trengths, **W**eaknesses, **O**pportunities, and **T**hreats to a project, program, and portfolio. Strengths and Weaknesses are internal to an organization and Opportunities and Threats are external.

T

Term	Description
Task	A small piece of work that when combined with related tasks form an activity. A task has specific parameters such as time, scope, budget, and resource requirements. Larger tasks can be further divided into sub-tasks with specific assignments. When working with non-project professionals, the terms task and activities are often used interchangeably. Also see Assignment, Activity, and Work Breakdown Structure.
Team Building	The process of creating effective teams by thoughtful team formation, establishing team ground rules, conflict resolution, and promotion of cooperation and collaboration.
Technical Debt	A concept that reflects the implied cost of additional rework caused by choosing an easy solution, instead of utilizing a better approach that would take longer.

Term	Description
Technique	A defined procedure to perform a particular task and activity, such as the execution or performance of an artistic work or a scientific procedure and often by using specific tools.
Test-Driven Development (TDD)	A software development process that relies on the repetition of a short development cycle that works in reverse, as opposed to the more traditional approaches. Instead of starting with requirements, this approach starts with real test cases of how the product would be used. By developing against the test cases, the goal is to achieve zero defects.
Threat	A risk that has the potential to influence negatively one or multiple portfolio, program, or project goals. See also Issue, Opportunity, and Risk.
Three-Point Estimating	An estimation technique used to approximate the outcome, such as costs or duration, by applying averages across optimistic, pessimistic, and realistic estimates. Also see Analogous Estimating, Bottom-up Estimating, Definitive Estimating, Parametric Estimating, and

Term	Description
	Program Evaluation and Review Technique (PERT).
Threshold	An upper or lower limit parameter used to indicate the maximum or minimum amount of time, cost, or other parameters in which an action or process may take place.
Time and Material Contract (T&M)	A contract type whereby the seller is paid for the time and material of the agreed upon work. The negative risk of work expansion is typically held by the buyer.
Timebox	A technique for fixing time in which a task or activity must be accomplished.
To-Complete Performance Index (TCPI)	An earned value management measurement of the cost performance that shows the ability to complete the remaining work with the remaining resources. It is expressed as the ratio of the cost to complete the remaining work to the remaining budget.
Tolerance	The permitted deviation from a predetermined quality requirement.
Tool	A tangible aid, such as a template or software, used in performing a task or activity to more effectively and

Term	Description
	efficiently produce a product or a result.
Total Float (TF)	The time duration for which an extension or delay can be incurred by a scheduled activity in terms of its early start date without posing any violation to a schedule constraint or causing a delay in the project completion date. See also Float and Free Float.
Trend Analysis	A mathematical technique that uses historical results to predict a future outcome. This is achieved by tracking variances in cost and schedule performance.
Trigger	An event or situation that causes something to start. For example, in risk management, a trigger is a leading indicator in which a risk's probability of occurrence has just increased.
Trigger Condition	A situation or event that plays the role of an indicator in terms of assessing the occurrences of a risk.

Term	Description
T-Shaped	A metaphor used in describing a person with one deep area of specialization and also broad abilities in other areas as required by the team. Also see Broken Comb and I-Shape.

U

Term	Description
User Experience Design (UX design)	A process of enhancing user satisfaction with a product by seeking and adopting user input that results in the improvement of usability, accessibility, and the general pleasure of interaction with the product.
User Story	An informal, natural language description of one or more features of a software system. User stories are designed to provide clarity and real-life use of how the user will interact with the system.
User Story Mapping	A visual exercise that helps product managers and their development teams to define the work that will create the most delightful user experience. It is used to improve teams' understanding of their customers and to prioritize work.

V

Term	Description
Validation	The action of validating a product or service to ensure it meets customer needs.
Value	Tangible, intangible, and sometimes abstract business gains and advantages that are associated with the sponsoring organization's strategy, goals, and objectives. Also see Benefit.
Value Management	A combination of planning tools and methods to find the optimum balance of a project, program, and portfolio benefit in relation to costs and risks.
Value Stream	Artifacts within the business architecture that allow a business to specify the value proposition derived by an external or internal stakeholder from an organization.
Value Stream Mapping	A lean management method for analyzing the current state and designing a future state, for the series of events that take a product or service from its beginning through to the

Term	Description
	customer, while reducing lean waste as compared to the current map.
Variance Analysis	A method for identifying the level and cause of difference between the actual and baseline performance.
Variance at Completion (VAC)	An estimation of the budget surplus or deficit which is measured by subtracting Estimate at Completion (EAC) from Budget at Completion (BAC). *Formula: VAC = BAC - EAC*
Vision	A description of the direction in which an organization is intended to move toward (e.g. "Where do we want to be?"). Also see Mission.

W

Term	Description
WBS Dictionary	A detailed document that supports the Work Breakdown Structure (WBS) by enlisting the details of the deliverable, activity, and scheduling information about WBS components. Also see Work Breakdown Structure (WBS).
Weighted Milestone Method	A technique for determining Earned Value by dividing the work package's budget value into portions that are measurable and concluding every portion with a milestone with which a weighted budget value is associated. See also Fixed Formula Method.
What-If Scenario Analysis	The method of determining the impact of scenarios on the organization, program, or project goals and/or objectives.
Work Breakdown Structure (WBS)	A hierarchical breakdown of the work scope required to be executed by the team for creating the deliverables and outcomes as well as for achieving the particular project goals and objectives.

Term	Description
	Also see Assignment, Activity, Organizational Breakdown Structure, Resource Breakdown Structure, Risk Breakdown Structure, Task, and WBS Dictionary.
Work Package	A small but measurable unit of work, typically at the lowest level of a work breakdown structure (WBS), in which there can be associated schedule, deliverable or outcome, quality attributes, resources to perform the work, risks, and issues. See also Work Breakdown Structure (WBS).
Workaround	An expedient response required to react quickly to an issue or situation. Workarounds are utilized when official and formal processes are either nonexistent, ineffective or unworkable.

Term	Description
Workplan (Schedule)	A Workplan is a tool used by the project team to plan, manage, report, and evaluate the progress of the initiative. It defines what work is to be accomplished, by whom, and when. It also identifies any predecessor and successor activities and tasks. The Workplan is a logical decomposition of the Work Breakdown Structure (WBS). Also see Work Breakdown Structure (WBS).

Common Project Management Formulas

Earned Value Formulas

Term	Acronym	Formula	Example[1]
Expected Monetary Value	EMV	Σ (prob. * impact)	$50,000
Budget at Completion, $	BAC, $		$50,000
Budget at Completion, Days	BAC, Days		100 Days
Planned Value	PV		$5,000
Earned Value	EV		$5,500
Actual Cost	AC		$4,500

Term	Acronym	Formula	Example[1]
Cost Variance	CV	EV - AC	$1,000
Schedule Variance	SV	EV - PV	$500
Cost Performance Index	CPI (>1 favorable)	EV / AC	1.22
Schedule Performance Index	SPI (>1 favorable)	EV / PV	1.10
Estimate at Completion	EAC	BAC / CPI or AC + ETC	$40,909
Estimate to Complete	ETC	EAC - AC	$36,409
Variance at Completion	VAC	BAC - EAC	$9,091
To-Complete Performance Index[2]	TCPI (<1 favorable)	A. (BAC-EV) / (BAC-AC) or B. (BAC-EV) / (EAC-AC)	0.98

Term	Acronym	Formula	Example[1]
Time Estimate at Complete	TEAC	BAC Days / SPI	90.9
Time Variance at Complete	TVAC	BAC Days - TEAC	9.1

[1]Example: Project X has a budget of $50,000 to be completed in 100 days. The planned burn rate is $500 per day on average. By Day 10, the project is clearly progressing faster, completing 10% more activities than planned and actually spent about 10% less budget than anticipated. At this point, the Earned Value calculations are shown in the Example column.

[2]TCPI has two formulas. Use A when the project is under budget. Use B when the project is overbudget. In the example above, the project is under budget (since CPI is greater than 1).

Financial Formulas

Term	Acronym	Formula
Benefit-Cost Ratio	BCR	Cash Flow / Project Investment
Future Value	FV	Present Value $(1 + r)^n$ r = Interest Rate n = number of periods
Internal Rate of Return	IRR	% Return on Project Investment
Net Present Value	NPV	PV Revenue – PV Cost
Payback Period	PP	Project Cost / Annual Cash Flow
Present Value	PV	Future Value $/ (1 + r)^n$ r = Interest Rate n = number of periods

Other Important Formulas

Term	Formula
Actual Average Burn Rate	EAC / (Actual Duration, Days)
Communication Channels	N (N − 1) / 2
Float	LF − EF or LS - ES
PERT	(P + 4M + O) / 6
Planned Average Burn Rate	(BAC, $) / (BAC, Days)
Risk Priority Number	Severity * Occurrence * Detection
Standard Deviation	(P − O) / 6
Variance	$\{(P - O) / 6\}^2$ or SD^2

For Our Readers

This terminology guide is a work-in-progress, and we plan to make regular updates. We welcome your suggestions for new terms and concepts that you consider to be widely popular. At the same, some of the terms in this current version may surely become less used over time. Also, as thorough as we try to be, there may be errors and omissions. We will be indebted to you for your input.

To view the most up-to-date glossary, visit www.ProjectManagement.co.

To submit your ideas of new terms or to update existing concepts, please submit your thoughts at
https://pmoadvisory.wufoo.com/forms/publication-feedback-form/

Thank you in advance for your help.

Special Offers

By registering this product, we will invite you to our monthly webinar and earn PDUs, all for free. We will also send occasional special offers for our training courses.

PMO Advisory's webinar presents current and hot topics in the world of project management. To see our webinar selections (past, present, and near future), visit www.pmoadvisory.com/webinar

To register this product, go to: www.pmoadvisory.com/about-pmo-advisory/product-registration/

9 781941 913093